D1402386

THE URAL MOUNTAINS

CHARLES W. MAYNARD

The Rosen Publishing Group's
PowerKids Press™
New York

+
947
MAY

For Elizabeth, Hal, and Will, friends who love walking mountain trails

Published in 2004 by The Rosen Publishing Group, Inc.
29 East 21st Street, New York, NY 10010

First Edition

Editor: Frances E. Ruffin
Book Design: Emily Muschinske
Photo Researcher: Barbara Koppelman

Photo Credits: Cover, pp. 4, 8 © John Cancalosi/Peter Arnold, Inc.; pp. 7 (top), 12 © Konrad Wothe/Minden Pictures; p. 7 (bottom) © James L. Amos/CORBIS; pp. 11, 15 (bottom) © Bryan & Cherry Alexander Photography; p. 15 (top) © Staffan Widstrand/CORBIS; p. 16 © 1996 CORBIS/courtesy of NASA/CORBIS; p. 16 (inset) © Margaret Bourke-White/Timepix; p. 19 © Reuters NewMedia Inc./CORBIS; p. 20 © Bios (M. Gunther/Peter Arnold, Inc.; p. 22 © Oyvind Ravna.

Manufactured in the United States of America

CONTENTS

4

CONTINENTAL BOUNDARY

The Ural Mountains form the **boundary** between the continents of Europe and Asia. The Urals extend 1,500 miles (2,414 km) from the Arctic Ocean in the north to the dry, treeless areas of land, called the **steppes**, in the country of Kazakhstan.

The Urals are low mountains with peaks averaging from 2,000 to 4,000 feet (610–1,219 m) above **sea level**. Gora Narodnaya lies in Russia's northern range of the Urals. It is known as the People's Mountain and is the highest peak in the Urals at 6,214 feet (1,894 m). East of the Urals lie the western Siberian lowlands. To the west is the European plain that runs from the Atlantic Ocean all the way to the foothills of the Urals. The Ural chain is divided into five regions. The mountains begin in Russia's treeless, frozen Arctic Urals and run south through the Sub-Arctic Urals, the narrow rocky North Urals, and through the tree-covered Middle and South Urals. The South Urals end in the country of Kazakhstan.

This is a view of a rocky mountain peak of the Ural Mountains in Russia's Siberian region.

ANCIENT MOUNTAINS

Earth's crust is made of **continental plates** that move slowly on Earth's surface. Over many millions of years, the plates pull apart in one direction and hit each other in another direction. When one plate bumps into another plate, Earth's surface wrinkles. This action creates a type of mountain called a fold mountain.

The Urals were folded from 300 to 250 million years ago when two plates collided, or bumped together, to form the land area Eurasia. The Urals are made of three kinds of rock, including **sedimentary rock** that was created on an ocean floor. Heat and pressure from the collision of the plates changed this sedimentary rock into harder **metamorphic rock**. Another kind of rock was formed when magma, or hot melted rock, came from cracks in the upper layers of Earth's crust. When the magma cooled, it formed even harder **igneous rock**.

MOUNTAIN FACT

MINING FOR PRECIOUS METALS, SUCH AS GOLD AND PLATINUM, AND FOR GEMSTONES, SUCH AS EMERALDS, TOPAZES, AND AMETHYSTS, IS AN IMPORTANT INDUSTRY IN THE URALS. THE SOUTH URALS ARE RICH IN IRON ORE.

Top: Koip Mountain is part of Russia's Ilych Mountain Reserve. Inset: Precious metals, such as platinum, are found in parts of the Urals.

Erosion has played a role in shaping and wearing down this mountain in the Urals.

After glaciers of frozen water and ice move down a mountain, they melt and form rivers, such as this winding river in Siberia.

WORN-DOWN PEAKS

Erosion has changed the shape and height of the peaks in the Urals over millions of years. Part of this process includes glaciers, rivers of ice that are built by yearly snowfalls. They become huge packs of ice that slowly move down mountains. As they move downhill, the glaciers pick up rocks and sand. Rocks, sand, and water carried by glaciers brush constantly against the mountain rock and cause mountains to wear down slowly.

Moving glaciers of water and ice have eroded the steep, sharp peaks of the Arctic and North Ural ranges. Glacier-carved valleys are *U* shaped, with steep sides and wide, flat bottoms. The Middle Urals and the South Urals have been eroded by water from snow melting to create streams and rivers. Water-carved valleys are *V* shaped, with narrow bottoms. Some of the rivers created by melting glaciers include Russia's Kama and Belaya Rivers, which flow into the Volga, the longest river in Europe. The Ural River flows from the mountains southward into the Caspian Sea, the world's largest lake.

Cold Climates

The climate in the Urals varies from a frozen Arctic Ocean climate to a dry, desert one in the southern region of the mountains. Climate is the kind of weather a certain area has. In most of the Urals, summers are short and winters are long. The **temperature** is above freezing, or more than 32°F (0°C), only 60 days per year. January's average daily high is -4°F (-20°C).

The highest peaks in the Arctic Urals stay covered with snow and ice year-round. There is snow throughout the winter, but it does not build up into deep snow. During the summer, the Arctic region averages a daily high temperature of 50°F (10°C) in July.

In the South Urals, snow covers mountain peaks in the south, but only during the cold winter months. Winter temperatures average 10°F (-12°C). Summers are longer in this region. The average daily high temperature in July is 72°F (22°C).

MOFANIZM

THE SOIL OF THE ARCTIC URALS AND THE NORTH URALS STAYS FROZEN. THIS FROZEN SOIL IS CALLED PERMAFROST. THE GROUND CAN BE FROZEN FROM 16 TO 20 FEET (5–6 M) DOWN BUT SOMETIMES IS FROZEN EVEN AS FAR AS 66 FEET (20 M) BELOW THE SURFACE. IT IS HARD TO BUILD ON PERMAFROST.

FACT

During winter the Nenet people live in tents made of reindeer skins. The Nenet people make their living by herding reindeer.

This is a summer day in western Siberia, Russia, where these children are playing on a homemade swing.

FORESTED SLOPES

The Arctic Urals are cold, treeless **tundra** covered mostly with ground-hugging plants such as mosses, and lichens, plants made of algae or fungi. In the Sub-Arctic and North Urals the rocky slopes of the mountains are alpine, or mountainous, tundra similar to the Arctic Urals. Its few trees are larch, spruce, Siberian fir, and birch. The Sub-Arctic **coniferous** forests just south of Siberia are called **taiga**.

The forest of the Yugyd Va National Park in northern Russia is an old-growth forest. This means the trees have not been cut there. It is the only old-growth forest still in Europe. This forest is also the only place to find the Siberian pine.

The Middle Urals are covered with thick, coniferous forests. Spruce and fir are the main trees there. The valleys are covered with rich soils for farming. The South Urals, with a milder climate, are heavily wooded with **deciduous** trees. The northern hardwood forests include beech, birch, maple and oak trees. The southern region's plateaus are broad, high, flat pieces of land. Cattle eat the grasses in the rich pastureland there.

 This forest of birch trees is located in the Pechora-Ilych Reserve area of the Ural Mountains. Inset: Blueberries and wildflowers grow in an ancient Ural forest.

Mountain Animal Life

The wildlife of the Urals is rich and varied. Many **mammals**, both large and small, live in the mountains. Smaller mammals include flying squirrels, beavers, otters, and weasels. Larger mammals are wolves, Arctic foxes, wolverines, lynxes, brown bears, moose, and elks. Reindeer, which were tamed about 2,000 years ago, are herded for their meat and for their hides, which provide clothing and tents for Arctic people. The large brown bear has come to stand for Russia. These bears are the same **species** as grizzly and Kodiak bears of North America. Brown bears can weigh from 209 to 1,716 pounds (95–778 kg). They live in the open tundra areas of the Urals. More than 200 species of birds live in the Urals, including black grouse, three-toed woodpeckers, nutcrackers, and teal ducks. Salmon, sturgeon, and whitefish are a few of the fish species that live in the rivers flowing from the Urals.

MOUNTAIN FACT

Caribou are also called reindeer. They live in the tundra of the North Urals. Caribou are from 34 to 55 inches (86–140 cm) tall at the shoulder and can weigh from 130 to 700 pounds (60 to 318 kg). Caribou eat mostly lichen, grasses, and tree roots.

A Nenet woman leads a train of reindeer on the ice-covered Ob River. Inset: These twin cubs are brown bears.

Mountains of Iron

The Urals run from north to south through Russia. At 6,592,800 square miles (17,075,400 sq km), the country has the largest area in the world. The major industries, or businesses, of the Urals are mining, producing metals, and cutting trees for **timber**. The vast mountain forests provide plenty of trees for the timber industry. The rich minerals have attracted miners for hundreds of years. Large factories make iron and steel from the iron ore of the Urals and the coal deposits of the nearby plains.

In the South Urals, the city of Magnitogorsk, Russia, was founded in 1929 as a tent city along the banks of the Ural River. The people living there produced steel during **World War II**. This city and others were important to Russia's war effort. Today the area continues to make iron and steel products. In the late 1800s, the Trans-Siberian Railroad was built through the Middle Urals. This railroad now travels 5,578 miles (8,977 km) from Moscow, the capital of Russia, to Vladivostok on the country's Pacific coast. It takes six days to travel from one end to the other.

The Trans-Siberian Railroad, shown in yellow, can be seen from space. Inset: These Russian workers produced steel during World War II in the city of Magnitogorsk.

PEOPLE OF THE URALS

People have lived in the Urals for thousands of years. **Primitive** hunters wandered through the mountains in search of game for food. The Komi, people who live in northwestern Russia, are **descendants** of ancient hunting and fishing tribes. Today many of the 300,000 Komi speak their own language and follow **traditions** that go back thousands of years. The Nenet people live near the Arctic Circle. Only 10,000 Nenet people still exist. They live in tents, travel from place to place, and herd reindeer.

Most of the people who live in the Urals are Russians. Many present-day Russians are descended from the **Vikings**, people who came from Sweden 1,000 years ago. The Vikings were called Rus because many had red hair. Russians conquered much of the European plain west of the Urals. In the 1700s and 1800s, their empire stretched across the Urals from Poland to Siberia.

MONGA FACT

In the southern ranges of the Ural Mountains live descendants of Genghis Khan. Khan was a feared chieftain from Mongolia who led his followers to conquer the steppes of Kazakhstan. These excellent horsemen lived in tents and traveled from place to place.

Hunters in Kazakhstan are excellent riders. They show off their skills by entering contests in which they ride their horses while holding golden eagles.

POLLUTION AND PROTECTION

The Urals are some of the oldest mountains on Earth, so **geologists** continue to study them. In 1995, scientists from Russia, Germany, Spain, and the United States went to the Urals to study the Ural Mountains. They hoped to understand better how mountains in other parts of the world were formed.

From the 1940s through the 1960s, industries and **nuclear** plants polluted the air, rivers, and soil of the region. The worst nuclear **contamination** in the world occurred near the city of Kyshtym, Russia, in 1949, 1957, and 1967, when nuclear wastes that were put into Lake Karachai made the water and soil **radioactive**.

Scientists are working to clean all types of pollution in the Urals. People are studying how best to clean harmful radioactive waste. They hope to make this part of the Urals a safe and beautiful place of snowy peaks, timbered slopes, clear lakes, and rushing streams.

Workers in Russia's Kiomi Republic struggle to clean oil from a leaking pipeline in a taiga forest. They hope to prevent further pollution of the environment that would harm the forest's plants and animals.

THE STONE BELT

The Urals, which are a long chain of stone mountains, have been called the Stone Belt. People have lived and hunted in this Stone Belt for many thousands of years. The Komi people began living in the Urals in the 900s. By the 1100s, Russian settlers from the west had moved into the valleys of the region. The first ironworks was built in the 1630s. In the late 1600s and the early 1700s, Peter the Great, the czar, or ruler, of Russia, encouraged the building of metal works. The making of metal grew into a major industry by the mid-1900s.

Miass, in the South Urals, is called the Town in the Golden Valley. A gold rush occurred there in the 1800s, after an 85-pound (39-kg) chunk of gold was believed to have been found there.

 This woman is a member of the Komi people who live in the Urals. She is wearing traditional Komi dress.

GLOSSARY

boundary (BOWN-duh-ree) The border that separates one area from another.

coniferous (kah-NIH-fur-us) Having cones and needlelike leaves.

contamination (kun-ta-mih-NAY-shun) The state of being made unfit for use.

continental plates (kon-tin-EN-tul PLAYTS) The moving pieces of Earth's crust.

deciduous (de-SIH-joo-us) Having leaves that fall off every year.

descendants (dih-SEN-dents) People who are born of a certain family or group.

erosion (ih-ROH-zhun) The wearing away of land over time.

geologists (jee-AH-luh-jists) Scientists who study the structure of Earth.

igneous rock (IG-nee-us ROK) Hot, liquid, underground rock that has cooled and hardened.

mammals (MA-mulz) Warm-blooded animals that have backbones and hair, breathe air, and feed milk to their young.

metamorphic rock (meh-tuh-MOR-fik ROK) Rock changed by heat and pressure.

nuclear (NOO-klee-ur) Having to do with the energy created by splitting atoms.

primitive (PRIH-muh-tiv) Something that is in an early stage of growth.

radioactive (ray-dee-oh-AK-tiv) Giving off rays of light, heat, or energy.

sea level (SEE LEH-vul) The height of the top of the ocean.

sedimentary rock (seh-dih-MEN-teh-ree ROK) Layers of gravel, sand, silt, or mud that have been pressed together to form rock.

species (SPEE-sheez) A single kind of animal or plant.

steppes (STEPS) Treeless lands with few plants, found in very cold places.

taiga (TY-guh) Forests with conifer trees that start where tundras end.

temperature (TEM-pruh-cher) How hot or cold something is.

timber (TIM-bur) Wood that is cut and used for building houses ships, and other wooden objects

traditions (truh-DIH-shunz) Ways of doing things that have been passed down over time.

tundra (TUN-druh) The frozen land of the coldest parts of the world.

Vikings (VY-kingz) Scandinavian sailors who attacked the coasts of Europe from the eighth to the tenth centuries.

World War II (WURLD WOR TOO) A war fought between the United States, Great Britain, France, and Russia and against Germany, Japan, and Italy from 1939 to 1945.

Index

Web Sites

Due to the changing nature of Internet links, PowerKids Press has developed an online list of Web sites related to the subject of this book. This site is updated regularly. Please use this link to access the list:
www.powerkidslinks.com/gmrw/uralmoun/